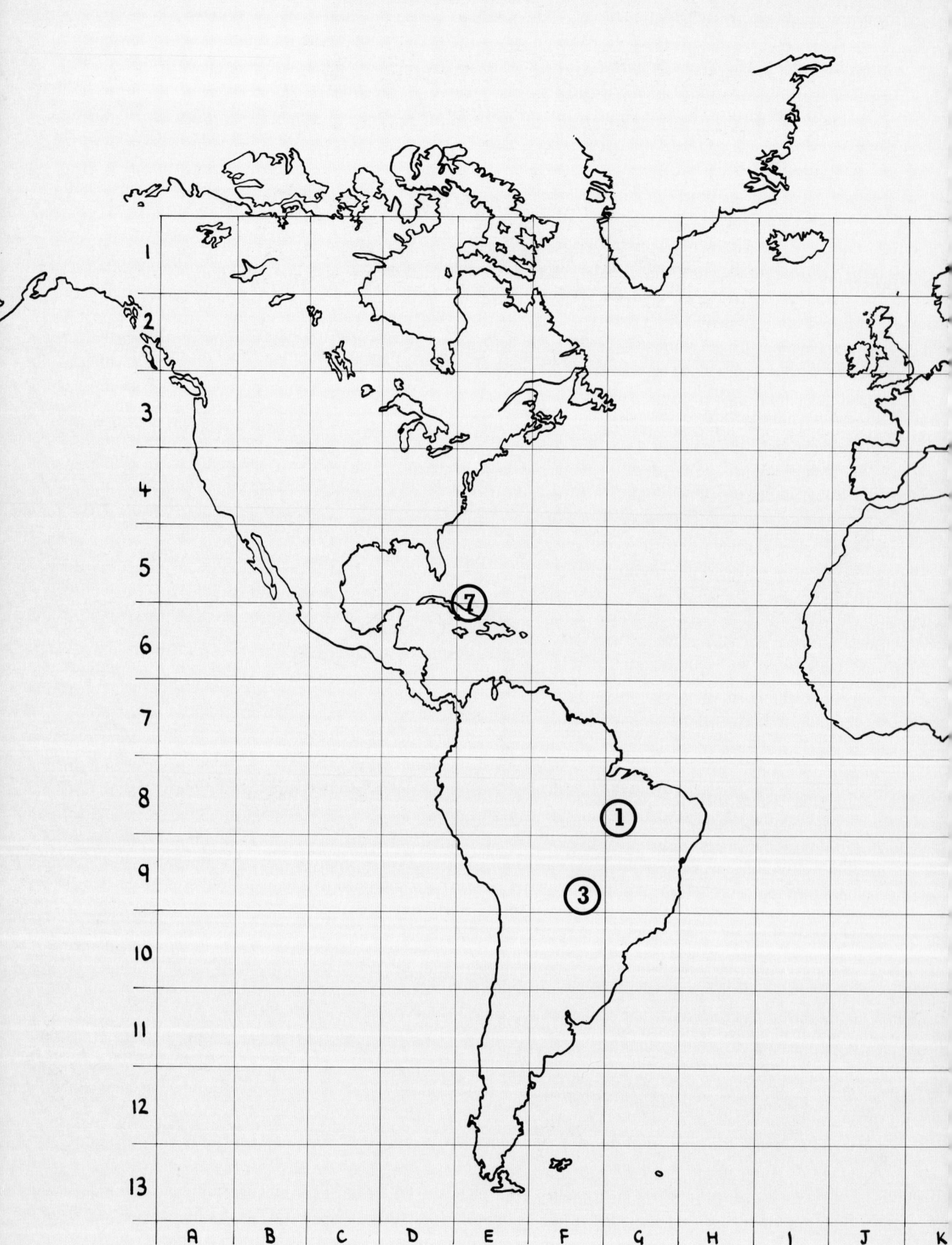

DAVID TAYLOR'S
ANIMALS IN DANGER

Authorised by 'D' for use
by agents of
CIA, KGB and MI5

Acknowledgements

The publishers would like to thank the following for permission to reproduce photographs in this book:

Ardea London Limited: pages 18 and 26.
Bruce Coleman Limited: pages 7 (LC Marigo), 8 (Jeff Foott), 9 WWF/H Jungius), 10 (Sullivan & Rogers), 11 (John Cancalosi), 15 (LC Marigo), 16r (Rod Williams), 17 (Mark Boulton), 19 (Christian Zuber), 21 (Bruce Coleman Limited), 22 (Jen & Des Bartlett), 24 (Michael Freeman), 25l (Jen & Des Bartlett), 25r (CB & DW Frith), 29 (John Wallis), 31 (John Visser), 32 (JLG Grande), 33 (John Topham), 34 (Gerald Cubitt), 35 (Stephen J Krasemann), 38 (Christian Zuber), 39 (Rod Williams), 40 (Norman Myers), 43 (John Cancalosi), 44 (John Cancalosi),
45 (John Anthony).
Oxford Scientific Film Stills: pages 12 and 16l.

First published in Great Britain in 1990 by Boxtree Limited
Text copyright © 1990 by David Taylor
Artwork copyright © by Boxtree Limited
Front cover illustration and all artwork by David Quinn
Typeset by York House Typographic Ltd
Origination by Culver Graphics
Designed by Groom & Pickerill
Printed in Singapore
for Boxtree Limited, 36 Tavistock Street,
London WC2E 7PB

British Library Cataloguing in Publication Data
Taylor, David, *1934–*
Animals in danger.
1. Animals in danger. extinction
I. Title   II. Quinn, David
591.529
ISBN 1-85283-037-9

CONTENTS

Introduction 6

TARGET 1 **Giant Otter** 7

TARGET 2 **Snow Leopard** 10

TARGET 3 **Rare Macaws** 13

TARGET 4 **African Wild Ass** 17

TARGET 5 **Komodo Dragon** 21

TARGET 6 **Okapi** 25

TARGET 7 **Cuban Crocodile** 28

TARGET 8 **African Hunting Dog** 33

TARGET 9 **Lemurs** 37

TARGET 10 **Gorilla** 41

Abbreviations
mm millimetre
cm centimetre
m metre
km kilometre
kmh kilometres per hour
ha hectare
gm gram
kg kilogram

Operation Minerva

TOP SECRET

Read, memorise and then destroy this document.

The location of the headquarters of The Organisation is known to only a few people. On the door as you arrive for briefing, you see the brass plate and its inscriptions in large letters:

CIA
(Campaign against Insensitivity towards Animals)

KGB
(Keen Guardian Biologists)

MI5
(Mammal Intelligence Unit 5)

After electronic screening, you are admitted to my office. The following conversation is recorded by my monitors:

'Good morning, my code name is **D**. Sit down, please, and let me outline the mission ahead of you.

'Conservation of wildlife, the protection of endangered species – all of us are familiar with, and whole-heartedly approve of, the idea. Every day we read in the newspapers of some threat – natural disasters or aspects of human activity – that are claiming the lives of some animal or plant that has survived on this planet for millions of years, but is now in imminent danger of vanishing for ever. Pandas starving when the bamboo flowers once in a hundred years, whales still hunted by the Japanese and Icelanders, rainforests burned deliberately to provide more space for cattle ranching, oil slicks and pesticides poisoning shellfish, sea birds and sea otters.

'Changes in the way man uses the world that he shares with other living creatures threaten not only famous species like rhinos and giant otters, but also many lesser known but equally fascinating animals that have their rightful place in the scheme of things – lizards, spiders, the minute creatures that make coral, and all sorts of rare insect.

'I have decided to enlist you in my elite intelligence service as an undercover agent. Your code name for the operation is Treble Zero, **000**. Your mission is to investigate and report on status, whereabouts, enemies of, ten "target" animals. They were last seen in different parts of the world. All are in danger, all need our help. You must set out, locate and assess the situation for each of the ten and then report back here to mission control. Your equipment – a map with grid references is provided at the beginning of this book – otherwise you must rely on your wits and physical fitness. Communicate on secure satellite channel 22. And leave your Biretta automatic behind!

'The risks: you are up against formidable opposition, the selfish human being in his many guises – governments, industrialists, criminals, the unthinking man in the street, often uninformed and frequently a source of pollution.

'Here are your dossiers containing key information on the targets. The operation is code-named "Minerva" after the Roman Goddess of Wisdom, whose symbol was the owl. The password – "**Owl-Hoot**".

'Good luck and good hunting, **000**!'

Degree of survival threat for each target is colour-coded as follows:

Red: Endangered and may soon be extinct in the wild.

Orange: Endangered and may soon be extinct in the wild. Some populations flourishing in captivity.

Yellow: At risk with numbers of animals falling rapidly.

Green: Some threat but not at present in danger of extinction.

OPERATION MINERVA:

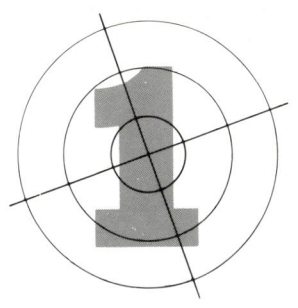

NAME ☐ Giant Otter

ALIAS ☐ *Pteronura brasiliensis*

REPORTED SEEN ☐ Map ref G8

BACKGROUND ☐ This beautiful animal can grow to a length of almost 2 m from nose to tail tip and weigh as much as 35 kg. It is the biggest, and probably the rarest, of all otters with a most handsome velvety, chocolate-brown coat that sports creamy white patches or streaks on the underparts, particularly the throat area. As a result the *giant otter* frequently looks as if he were wearing a white tie, cravat or necklace to accompany a smart brown suit; hence one of its local names is 'Lobo corbata' – which means 'wolf with a tie'!

Other locations where it can be seen ☐
Zoos at MADRID (Spain), DUISBURG (Germany).

Estimated degree of survival threat ☐
Condition orange. Numbers declining over most of its range.

Field report from 000 to D.
Operation Minerva. Top priority.
24 August. 06.00 hrs.
Have located the giant otter. Once the species was to be found over most of the north-eastern and central areas of South America, but in many places it has completely disappeared or been reduced to small scattered populations, sometimes numbering 20, but more usually less.
Details ☐ Otters are amphibious carnivores belonging to the weasel family of mammals which also includes skunks,

The giant otter of South America is a master swimmer.

mink and badgers. There are 12 species of otter living in various parts of the world. Only one species is wholly marine, seldom coming ashore – the delightful *sea otter* which loves to float on its back in the water, cracking shellfish on its chest with its nimble forepaws. The others mess about mainly or exclusively in freshwater rivers, lakes and streams.

Otters are intelligent, inquisitive, playful, hyper-active animals. They are brilliant swimmers, being equipped with a streamlined body, tightly packed waterproof body hair, webbed feet in most species, including the giant, and a strong rudder-like tail which is somewhat flattened. They feed on water-living creatures which they find by using their eyes, touch and vibration-responsive whiskers and, in those otters which do not have claws, sensitive 'finger' tips. Even the smaller kinds of otter have a powerful

A seafood lunch in the sunny Pacific – a sea otter munches abalone.

bite and I have seen terrible wounds inflicted on humans who took liberties with them.

Giant otters chase fish under water and also catch crabs. They hunt mainly by day, and after catching their prey with their mouths, hold it in their forepaws and eat its head first, often while lounging in shallow water. They live in slow-running rivers, creeks, lakes and marshes in forested areas. When the rivers flood the forest during the rainy season, the fish go with the flood water to spawn and the otters follow.

These beautiful creatures form strong pair-bonds, with the female usually being the boss! They are territorial animals, marking their property with droppings (spraints) and urine left at specific places which they clear of vegetation to make a

The endangered giant otter has caught his dinner.

A pair of giant otters bask on a log beside the Amazon.

flat half-circle. They 'garden' the marked areas regularly to keep them tidy and free from overgrowth of plants. Giant otter groups have communal lavatories where urine and droppings are mixed with the soil or mud by thorough kneading with the front and hind paws.

Giant otters can be quite noisy. They have a wide repertoire of sounds which they can use for communication, and I have heard humming noises, whistles, squeals, coos, growls and barks.

Litters of one to five, but usually two, cubs are born in a holt (den) burrowed into a river bank, after a pregnancy of 65-70 days. Giant otters can live for about 12 years in the wild and much longer in zoos. *Message ends.*

D to 000. How many giant otters do you estimate still exist?

000 to D. Numbers unknown, but undoubtedly falling rapidly.

D to 000. Please identify enemies of giant otter.

000 to D. Re. Giant otter enemies.
1. Man. Hunting the otter to provide pelts for the fur trade was, and still remains, a major threat. Approximately 2,000 skins a year were at one time being exported from Brazil alone. Although hunting bans were introduced in the 1970s, much illegal poaching continues. Once again the fur trade has a lot to answer for.
2. Man. Destruction of forests for timber and to exploit land for agriculture and mining, as well as the draining of vast areas, has severely affected the availability of the shallow creeks and seasonal flooding that are so important to the giant otter lifestyle.
3. Competition from the spread of four still numerous smaller species of otter that live in South America may also be important. *Message ends.*

D to 000. What other species of otter are also under significant threat?

000 to D. As well as the giant otter, the *marine otter* of South American coastlands is in danger, but many others, including the *Eurasian* and *North American otters* are also at risk as habitat destruction and water pollution take their toll.

Report ends: file **urgently**.

OPERATION MINERVA: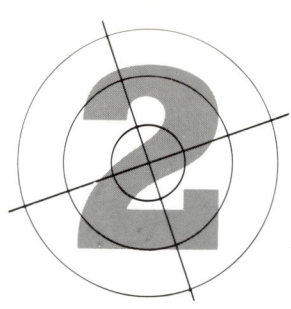

NAME □ Snow Leopard

ALIAS □ *Panthera uncia*
Also known as ounce. This name was once also applied to the lynx and the cheetah and is derived from the Latin word for lynx.

REPORTED SEEN □ Map ref P5

BACKGROUND □ Not much is known about this target. D is particularly fond of the cat family and considers this species to be the most glamorous and spectacular of all. It is a little smaller than a leopard, weighing 65-75 kg, with wonderfully long, dense fur of a smoky blue-grey colour tinged with pale yellow lightening to white on the underparts. The head and lower limbs display round black spots and the backs of the ears are black. The body markings are large, rather fuzzy rosettes among which are small dense black spots. The tail is relatively larger than that of a leopard, luxuriously furred and patterned with rings of dark rosettes. The pads of the paws are sensibly provided with furry

The most beautiful of all cats – a pair of snow leopards.

'snowshoes' which insulate them against the cold and also increase the weight-bearing area of the feet — useful when padding about in soft snow.

The *snow leopard* was first heard of by Europeans in 1761 when a French naturalist confused it with the cheetah by wrongly saying that it came from Persia where it was trained for hunting.

Other locations where it can be seen ☐
Many zoos including PORT LYMPNE, EDINBURGH and MARWELL (UK), BASLE (Switzerland), CHICAGO, CINCINNATTI (USA).

Estimated degree of survival threat ☐
Condition orange-red. Luckily it is breeding regularly in many zoos.

Special warning to investigating agents ☐
Take great care in approaching poachers of this animal — they are armed and known to react usually with violence.

Field report from 000 to D.
Top priority. Operation Minerva.
13 September. 09.45 hrs.
Have located the snow leopard with great difficulty and after much effort. It inhabits the high mountains of Afghanistan, and east to Siberia and Tibet, sometimes going up to the snowfields above 5,000 m. It is a shy, secretive cat adapted to life in a harsh environment. In winter it can be found at lower levels (2,000-3,000 m) in forests, where it follows its prey animals as they migrate down below the tree-line.

The snow leopard is a tough and highly agile cat that can make great leaps of up to 15 m. It is basically nocturnal, but frequently hunts by day and is particularly fond of the rugged but nimble ibex. It also takes wild sheep, musk deer, wild boar, small mammals like marmots and pikas, birds and, from time to time in the winter, domestic animals. Snow leopards are keen stalkers and setters of ambushes and they regularly patrol high points in the mountains from which they can survey the terrain below. Like domestic cats, they love to roll about in the plant called catnip. They do not roar like lions but can purr, and like smaller felines they feed while in a crouched position. They possess a round eye pupil rather than a slit.

Usually solitary animals, snow leopards travel long distances throughout their immense territories, leaving typical feline 'markers' in the form of rocks and tree trunks sprayed with pungent urine, and also scratch marks on the ground. They shelter in a cleft in a rock or beneath an overhanging boulder, and in some areas take over the huge nests built by vultures in low trees. Pity the poor vulture that tries to evict a squatting snow leopard from its property!

Pregnancy in a female snow leopard lasts about 100 days, after which a litter of one to four young are born, normally in the spring or early summer. The mother delivers the cubs in a den, comfortably lined with her own moulted fur to a depth of 1-1.5 cm. The cubs weigh four to seven times as much as a newborn domestic kitten at birth. They open their eyes at about one week of age, first eat solids when they are one month old and are weaned at two to two and a half months. The young cubs stay with their mothers for about nine months.

The snow leopard's gorgeous coat led to it being hunted by man.

No snow leopard has ever attacked a human being unless severely provoked. In zoos they have lived for up to 15 years. *Message ends.*

D to 000. Please identify enemies of snow leopard.

000 to D. Re. snow leopard enemies.
1. Man. Unscrupulous hunters still covet this animal because of its beautiful coat and the fur trade continues to connive with them in order to supply vain and stupid women with snow leopard pelts. Although snow leopard hunting is illegal in most countries where it exists, poaching and trapping continues, particularly in Afghanistan and Kashmir. It is relatively easy to purchase snow leopard furs in Kashmir, a part of the animals' range where human persecution is particularly severe.
2. In some areas the natural prey of the snow leopard is disappearing as mountain pastures are developed for the grazing of domestic farm livestock. Consequently the snow leopard population simultaneously decreases. *Message ends.*

D to 000. Message received and understood. The fur trade in some countries is obviously still a prime offender. Hopefully governments will clamp down more firmly on exports and imports of snow leopard furs. If so-called 'fashionable' people refused to wear the fur, trade in it would cease and this magnificent cat of the remote Asian mountains might be safe from extinction.

Snow leopard cubs love to play just like domestic kittens.

A moment of extreme danger for a beautiful snow leopard.

OPERATION MINERVA: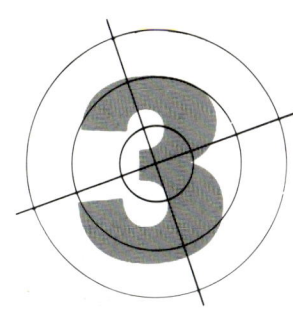

NAME □ Rare Macaws

ALIASES □ *Anodorhynchus hyacinthinus, Cyanopsitta spixii* etc.

REPORTED SEEN □ Map ref F9

BACKGROUND □ There are 328 species in the Psittacine family of birds which includes parrots, cockatoos and lories. One of them of course is the friendly budgerigar. The parrots of the New World first became known to Europeans in the fifteenth and sixteenth centuries when Spanish, Portuguese and English explorers began to penetrate South America, although Old World psittacines had been kept as talking pets in Greece since at least 400 BC. By the way, Shakespeare mentioned parrots in *The Merchant of Venice*; 'nature hath framed strange fellows in her time:

Forest destruction threatens rare parrots such as these hyacinthine macaws.

Some that will evermore peep through their eyes, And laugh like parrots at a bagpiper . . .'

Macaws are the largest and most spectacular members of the family. Like all parrots, they have the typical and familiar bill with the two curved mandibles, the upper of which is larger and more hooked than the lower one over which it fits. This bill is immensely powerful in macaws and can crack open Brazil nuts, inflict deep wounds on prying human fingers and also be employed as a useful climbing hook to assist the feet. The tongue is stubby, thick and muscular and contains a little bone. Note also the toes of parrots – unlike the arrangement in other birds, the two outer toes point backwards and the two inner ones point forwards. The foot of a parrot can not only be used for perching and climbing, but also as a most dextrous hand for grasping and manipulating things.

Incidentally, parrots are naturally either 'left-handed' or 'right-handed', and favour using one foot or the other, just like humans do with their hands. No other kind of bird is so 'handy' and skilled in using its feet as are parrots – not even the powerfully taloned eagles and hawks.

Macaws are vividly coloured birds, some of them bedecked in breathtaking multi-hued plumage. Although big, these strong birds are fast fliers.

Many species are endangered and some are on the verge of extinction. Your mission is to get at the facts about these very 'pretty pollies'.

Other locations where they can be seen □

Zoos, bird gardens and private aviaries.

Estimated degree of survival threat □

Condition green to red depending on species.

Field report from 000 to D.

Top priority. Operation Minerva.
4 October. 10.25 hrs.

There are many different species of macaw living in this part of the New World. They do *not* occur in the wild in Africa or Asia. Some are relatively small, like *Hahn's macaw*, which weighs about 165 g, while others are far bigger, the biggest being the *hyacinthine macaw* which tips the scales at up to 1.5 kg.

Like most other parrots of the region, macaws eat nuts, seeds and fruit, dwell in the trees of the rainforest, and nest in holes in tree trunks, either completely making the holes themselves or enlarging the holes made by other bird species. You can't tell a male from a female macaw just by looking at them – they appear identical (at least to the human eye!). Veterinary surgeons using a technique called endoscopy can find out which is which.

Female macaws lay two to four eggs, incubating them themselves for about 26 days, though the male does fuss about quite a lot in the nest during this time. It takes from three to three and a half months for the macaw chicks to grow their plumage (fledge) while they remain in the nest.

The kind of macaw kept as a pet, often seen in zoos and one of the most numerous in the wild, is the *blue and yellow*. It sports a bright blue back and wings with buttercup yellow underparts, and has a white face marked with black lines. Other

The useful grasping foot of a macaw.

macaws you will surely see in aviaries are the *scarlet* and the *green-winged*.

But the central targets of my mission are the much rarer, more endangered macaws. It has been incredibly difficult to locate them. The largest of the macaws, the hyacinthine, possesses, not surprisingly, the biggest and strongest bill of any parrot. It could nip off your thumb with the greatest of ease. A marvellous lilac hyacinth colour, with bright yellow skin surrounding the eyes and the lower mandible, it is a stunning bird that lives in parts of the Brazilian, Paraguayan and Bolivian rainforest. Its numbers in the

A pair of hyacinthine macaws at their nest in the Brazilian rainforest.

The handsome scarlet macaw can often be seen in zoos and bird gardens.

wild are declining fast. Even rarer is the *Lear's macaw*, a smaller version of the hyacinthine, first discovered in 1978. Only one population of fewer than 100 birds is now thought to survive. Another parrot that resembles the Lear's, called the *glaucous macaw*, is probably already extinct.

Spix's macaw, the only macaw with a completely feathered head (all the others have bare faces) is blue with a grey head. Its home is the forest of north-eastern Brazil, but the number of birds in the wild is probably less than half a dozen – if that! Spix's macaw is without doubt the most endangered of all the parrots in South America. Very few are in captivity (about 20 in total worldwide) and there has been virtually no breeding so far. *Message ends.*

D to 000. Please identify enemies of the rare macaws.

000 to D. Re. Macaw enemies.
1. Man. Over the years birds have been taken from the wild in vast and irresponsible numbers for the pet trade and to supply zoos and aviaries. Many countries have now brought in laws to stop this trade and there are international agreements to enforce them. Sadly some governments and customs services only pay lip-service to the protective legislation. Corruption, illegal poaching and smuggling continue to reduce the wild macaw populations, with many thousands of dollars being paid for specimens of the rarer species. Happily, lots of macaws are reproducing well in zoos and bird gardens, but some, such as the Spix's, are not, and may well soon disappear for ever.
2. Man. Destruction of the rainforest has eliminated the habitats of many parrot species including macaws such as the hyacinthine. While some parrots can adapt to life in the agricultural landscape that has replaced the Amazonian jungle in many areas, others, less versatile in their lifestyles, cannot and simply fade away. *Message ends.*

Fewer than a hundred of the very rare Lear's macaw now exist.

OPERATION MINERVA: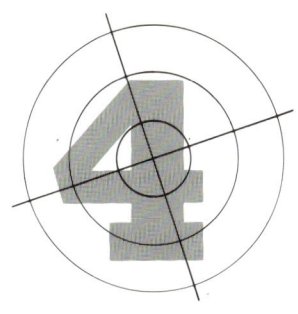

NAME □ African Wild Ass

ALIASES □ African wild donkey, *Equus africanus*.

REPORTED SEEN □ Map ref M6

BACKGROUND □ This mission is deadly serious, despite the fact that you might at first think the target is just another *donkey*. Everyone loves donkeys, but they are hardly rare or endangered (except in the sense that those rescued by donkey sanctuaries or the Horses and Ponies Protection Association are).

Ass is frequently used as an alternative name for donkey, and the animal you will seek in this phase of your mission is an ass and, further, the kind of ass from which the familiar domestic donkey is descended.

Ass, as you know only too well, is a common derogatory term for a stupid person. You may recall that Mr Bumble, the beadle in Charles Dickens' *Oliver Twist*, declared that 'the law is an ass – an idiot'. On the other hand, the ass or donkey has had its moments of great glory and importance; Jesus rode on one into Jerusalem on Palm Sunday; in Islam it is said that one of the ten animals to be admitted into heaven besides man is Balaam's ass, the one that spoke, mentioned in the Old

It's easy to see the relationship between the wild ass (here pictured) and the friendly donkey.

Testament of the Bible; and the ass was the symbol of one of the lost tribes of Israel.

Your target is no stubborn, stupid moke, much as it may look like one. It is in fact a fine, tough, intelligent and very rare species.

The *African wild ass* is bigger than most domestic donkeys, with long donkey-like ears, a grey body colour that shades to white on the underparts, white legs and a white muzzle. There is a thin black stripe along the back together with either a transverse stripe at the shoulder to make the cross design seen in ordinary donkeys or zebra-striped legs. The tail is tufted and the mane is thin, short and upright, 'punk-fashion'!

Other locations where it can be seen ☐
THE HAI BAR RESERVE in Israel, STUTTGART, WEST BERLIN (Germany), BASLE (Switzerland), SAN DIEGO (USA).

Estimated degree of survival threat ☐
Condition red.

The wild ass at home in typical terrain.

Field report from 000 to D.
Operation Minerva.
14 November. 09.00 hrs.
This has been my toughest assignment so far, entailing arduous journeys into the hottest, most arid places in the desert.

There are two races of African wild ass, the *Nubian* and the *Somali*. Both inhabit the most inhospitable terrain, where temperatures of 50°C (122°F) during the daytime are common. The asses live in herds of up to about ten animals, usually led by an old female, while the older males live separately. They somehow survive on what little desert vegetation they can find, grazing from dawn till mid-morning, resting during the heat of the day in the shade of a bush or a rocky hillock, and then feeding again from about 5 o'clock until sunset. During the night they sometimes trek long distances to water holes, but regularly go without for two days!

They are splendid beasts – masters of the desert. They run fast (up to at least 48 kmh) – and can spot trouble a long way off. Shy and cautious, they are quick to run for safety, but stop every now and then to look back and check whether they are being pursued. If cornered, they will

A young wild ass prepares to drink.

fight valiantly, kicking and biting hard and fast. No placid seaside, beach-plodding donkeys these!

Once, the wild ass was to be found across much of North Africa and there are ancient rock-face paintings of them still to be seen in Algeria. The wild ass has evolved, as you might expect, from the same ancestors as the horse. The details of their family tree are complex and still not completely worked out.

About 55 million years ago, in what are now called Europe and North America, but were then joined together in one land mass, a little dog-like animal moved through the forests, browsing on low shrubs. This was *Hyracotherium*, ancestor of the horses and also of the rhinoceroses and tapirs. Descended itself from forebears possessing the basic five toes per foot, it had already lost two outer toes on its hind feet and one inner toe on its fore feet, the remaining toes looking doglike, with pads; there was no sign of hooves as yet. It had a short muzzle and a long tail held curved like a cat's. As the

ages passed, the descendants of *Hyracotherium* split off into numerous branches of the family tree. The rhinos and tapirs went their way; the equine branch went theirs, discarding more toes so that they might concentrate on perfecting a single, highly modified toe on each foot, growing larger, developing teeth that were ideal for cropping and grinding grass, and acquiring large, efficient eyes.

By about one million years ago, all the surviving equine descendants of *Hyracotherium* had settled into four main groups; the horses, the asses, the half-asses and the zebras. These four groups were distributed in fairly specific parts of Africa, Europe and the Middle East, with almost no overlapping of the various groups. The zebras were purely Southern African and the half-asses (ancestors of the onager, kulan, kiang and djiggetai, and of the hemione which became extinct about one hundred years ago) were all Asiatic. The asses, from which donkeys later developed, were purely northern African and the horses (including ponies, which are simply horses under 14.2 hands high) were inhabitants of Europe and Western Asia.

Drought and civil war have been the principal enemies of the tough wild ass.

At the present time probably only 2-3,000 wild asses exist, though the military and political situation in Ethiopia may well have reduced that number drastically in recent years. *Message ends.*

D to 000. Please identify enemies of African wild ass.

000 to D. Re. wild ass enemies.
1. Man. Although supposedly protected in the areas where they exist, there is little doubt that the conditions of civil war in parts of Ethiopia and elsewhere in the wild asses' range, have resulted in the deaths of untold numbers of these animals.
2. The terrible drought which in recent years has resulted in so much human famine in Ethiopia, the Sudan etc., has also taken its toll of animals. *Message ends.*

OPERATION MINERVA: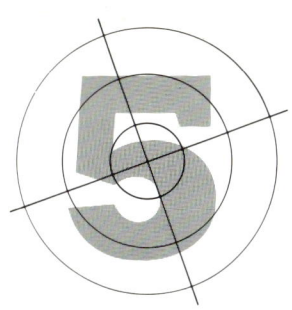

NAME □ **Komodo Dragon**

ALIASES □ Ora (the proper local name for this lizard), *Varanus komodoensis*.

REPORTED SEEN □ Map ref T6

BACKGROUND □ Rare, fascinating and dangerous, having been known to kill human beings on many occasions, this largest of living lizards lives on only Flores Komodo, Rintja and three other much smaller Indonesian islands in the Lesser Sunda group.

It can grow to over 3 m and specimens of perhaps as long as 5 m may have existed within living memory.

Depending on how full its stomach is, a 3 m long specimen can weigh between 100 and 250 kg, nothing compared with its even bigger relative that lived one million years ago and topped 2 tonnes!

An adult *Komodo dragon* has a stocky body and stout legs covered by scaly skin of an almost uniform grey colour whose texture reminds me of the outside of a lychee fruit, finely pimply rather than smooth and shiny like a snake. Young dragons are speckled and come in a variety of yellowish and greenish hues. The mouth carries a formidable array of backward-curved teeth designed for cutting flesh, and there is a bright yellow tongue that does the tasting, not

The flicking tongue of a dragon works much like that of a snake.

only of solids, but also, more importantly in such reptiles, of the air around it.

I have worked with these giant lizards and consider them to be more intelligent than most other reptiles; they really seem to watch you purposefully with their gleaming eyes. But be careful, 000, they can be very aggressive and may move surprisingly quickly. If you get into trouble, remember you're on your own!

Other locations where it can be seen ☐
Zoos at MADRID (Spain), ANTWERP (Belgium), SYDNEY (Australia), SAN DIEGO (USA).

Estimated degree of survival threat ☐
Condition yellow.

Field report from 000 to D.
Top priority. Operation Minerva.
3 January. 09.00 hrs.
The Komodo dragon is remarkable in having the smallest range of any of the large carnivores on this planet. In its island homes, some of which are very

Three Komodo dragons share a meal.

mountainous and volcanic, it mainly stays in the lowland, occasionally wandering as high as 2,000 m. A good swimmer, it can dive to 2 m and can cross small expanses of sea to reach other islands. Its typical environment is dry savannah land and the woodland that surrounds it. Woodland fires are often deliberately started by the human inhabitants for agricultural purposes, but the dragon itself doesn't seem much affected by them. It escapes by running off or retreating to its burrow.

Komodo dragons dig burrows in open hillsides or the banks of dry creek beds, but use them infrequently. The burrows are only a few metres deep and the lizards lie in them curled up like hairpins. They are active mainly by day, although they

A Komodo dragon in its lair.

A successful ambush on a young deer.

do occasionally hunt by the light of a full moon. Being big, they can store heat in their bodies and, although 'cold-blooded' are less dependent on surrounding temperature than smaller reptiles in order to keep active.

Of all their senses, scent is the most highly developed and important. Their power of sight enables them to recognise people up to about 6 m away and food at perhaps 50 m. They do not hear very well.

Among other species their enemies include the domestic dog, monkeys, wild boar, civet cats, birds of prey and some snakes which eat young dragons. More important is cannibalism among themselves. Hungry dragons – and they are often very hungry – eat their fellows, particularly smaller individuals. If a dragon can survive all that, he stands a chance of reaching the age of about 50 years.

Female dragons lay eggs in tree stumps or, more usually, holes excavated in the ground. One to 30 (usually about 15) eggs with soft, smooth, leathery shells (approximately 9 x 5 cm) are laid between July and early September. They hatch eight to eight and a half months later.

These giant lizards are essentially scavengers who search for dead animals using their sense of smell/taste. They compete with dogs, wild boar and birds for the corpses of deer and other animals. Only the dog dare challenge the dragon over ownership of a corpse – and then the dragon almost always has the last word. Sometimes the dragons will dig up human corpses from their graves and eat them!

The cutting teeth of this lizard and its great muscular power as it shakes its head to and fro after taking hold of an item of food, enable it to rip off enormous chunks of meat. It can crunch easily through bone and can swallow half a deer or the entire leg of a goat at one gulp. One 2.5 m long dragon was seen to swallow a 15 kg pig whole and three or four adult dragons can consume all of a large water buffalo in three to five days. When hungry they will eat small deer antlers or the horns of goats, and bones are no problem for them.

But these hungry reptiles are also predators who seek *living* prey. They ambush or trail deer, wild pigs and farm animals, probably aided by their keen sense of

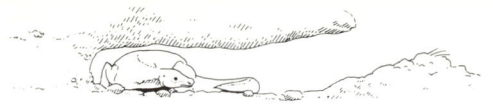

Although unable to breathe fire, this dragon has a powerful bite.

smell. With large animals like buffaloes, they can inflict serious wounds which lead later to the death of the victim, an event patiently awaited by the lizard who tracks down the corpse with the aid of that ever-flicking tongue.

They lay their ambushes for wild boar at the side of the game trails regularly used by these animals, or at waterholes. There are many reports from villagers in the islands claiming that lizards are particularly attracted to mares, cattle and goats when they are heavily pregnant. They hang around in the hope of grabbing a newborn animal or, some scientists speculate, hope that their presence will trigger a miscarriage and that they can then carry off the foetus.

Komodo dragons frequently enter villages to take domestic animals and a number of attacks on human beings are reported, including the deaths of two tourists within recent years. *Message ends.*

D to 000. How many Komodo dragons do you estimate still to exist?

000 to D. Probably 4-5,000.

D to 000. Please identify enemies of the Komodo dragon.

000 to D. Re. Komodo dragon enemies. The Indonesian government is enforcing protection of the Komodo dragons with much effort, but there remain:

1. Man. Illegal capture and killing. Sometimes villagers put poison in dead animals as bait for the lizards in order to get rid of them.
2. Starvation. Reduced availability of prey due to over-hunting of deer by man and changes in agricultural practice which have increased the numbers of farm livestock and further decreased the numbers of deer. Deer are the Komodo dragon's favourite prey.
3. Competition from feral (domestic animals gone back to the wild) dogs.
4. Uncontrolled burning of woodland reduces prey animals.

At present the position of the Komodo dragon is stable, but it remains highly vulnerable. *Message ends.*

OPERATION MINERVA:

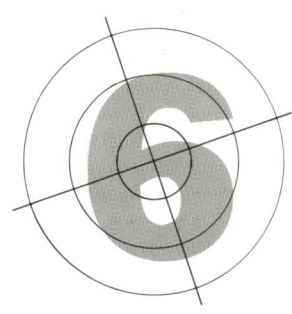

NAME □ Okapi
ALIAS □ *Okapia johnstoni*
REPORTED SEEN □ Map ref L7

BACKGROUND □ Your target in this instance is a most mysterious and elusive character. Western scientists first heard of its existence in 1901, when a British explorer, Johnstone, went in search of the horse-like animal that the pigmy people called 'okapi'. He found it living in the deep rainforest. A zoologist who examined the first bits of skin of the animal that were sent back to London, thought it was a new species of zebra and gave it the Latin name *Equus* (horse) *johnstoni*.

The shy okapi is the giraffe's closest living relative.

A remarkable and attractive creature, the *okapi* is the giraffe's closest living relative, though I find it to be more placid by nature than the latter. It wears a luxurious velvety chocolate-coloured coat of short hair with a gleaming sheen. The males have skin-covered peg-like 'horns' similar to those of giraffes and the head is rather giraffe-shaped, as is the neck, though much shorter in length. Again, like the giraffe, the okapi's 'fang' (canine) teeth are splayed out into lobes designed to strip the leaves off shoots when browsing, the tongue is long, extendible and dark grey, for grasping and plucking foliage, and, though there is none of the patched skin decoration of the giraffe, there are creamy coloured stripes on the legs and buttocks. Altogether the skin coloration and patterning is perfect camouflage for life in deep jungle conditions. The animals have large mobile ears and large dark eyes, both employed effectively in detecting approaching danger. Bull okapis stand about 1.7 m high and weigh up to 300 kg. The cows are a little bigger than the bulls.

Basically we know very little about the ways of the okapi in its native haunts – not surprising in view of the difficulty of studying it in the gloom of the dense forest. We don't even know how threatened it is. Some scientists

The remarkably long tongue of the okapi is great for cleaning the face.

The okapi's longish neck enables it to browse on trees.

Foolishly ate some soft fruit washed in village well water. Had my camera stolen while I was down with the fever.

Field report from 000 to D.
After many days hacking through almost impenetrable jungle and making enquiries at innumerable villages I have located the target here in Zaire.

Okapis inhabit relatively discrete areas of remote jungle, usually of secondary tree growth, with one or two animals living solitary lives per square kilometre of territory. They browse on low bushes of all kinds, taking young shoots, leaves and fruit. They have their own preferred pathways through the bush linking feeding zones, and mark their 'property' by leaving secretions on the ground from glands between their toes (giraffes do not possess these) and by urinating on bushes and trees. Probably each territory is the domain of a particular male okapi with females moving from one territory to another.

Like giraffes, okapis can live for over 30 years. Normally silent animals except when tending their young, the females call during the mating period which lasts about one month. Male okapis indulge in courtship displays that include head tossing, lip-curling and flicking of the legs. Sometimes two bulls will do battle over a female, either in ritual form, 'necking' like giraffe bulls do by pressing their necks together in a contest of strength, or more seriously by actually charging and butting one another.

Pregnancy in the female okapi lasts just over $14\frac{1}{2}$ months after which a single calf is born, usually in the rainy season. Curiously, and I think uniquely among mammals, the calf does not have its first bowel movement until 10-14 days after birth – this appears quite normal and harmless. Unlike the adults, the calf possesses a narrow stiff black mane and relatively thicker legs and smaller head and neck. It stays hidden in the undergrowth for the first month of its life, relying on its camouflage to hide it from important pre-

think it is in danger, but without being in risk of imminent extinction. Go to it, 000 (don't forget to have your yellow fever vaccination and take your anti-malaria pills).

Other locations where it can be seen □
Zoos in BRISTOL (UK), BASLE (Switzerland), CHICAGO, COLORADO and DALLAS (USA).

Estimated degree of survival threat □
Condition yellow.

D to 000. *2 February. 09.00 hrs.* Am still awaiting your report, now one month overdue.

000 to D. *Top priority. Operation Minerva. 4 February. 22.00 hrs.* Have been laid up with typhoid fever.

dators such as the leopard, and exchanging low bleating or whistling sounds with its mother from time to time. If a leopard does attack a calf, the parent will attempt to drive it off with powerful kicks of the legs.

Recently some scientists have suggested that the okapi may not be as closely related to the giraffe as has been generally thought, and that its nearest 'kith and kin' may be the *nilgai*, the large 'horse antelopes' that live in India and do look a bit okapi-like to me. *Message ends.*

D to 000. How many okapi do you estimate still to exist?

000 to D. Number totally unknown. There may be hundreds or perhaps a few thousand.

The beautiful okapi is well camouflaged for the deep jungle.

D to 000. Please identify enemies of the okapi.

000 to D. Re. okapi enemies.
1. Man, the hunter. Although the okapi has been protected by law since 1933 in this country, it is extremely difficult, because of the terrain, to prevent illegal hunting. For thousands of years pygmies who also live in this region have hunted okapis as part of their unending struggle to survive in the jungle, and they pose no threat to the survival of the species. It is men from outside, the greedy commercial poachers, killing the okapi to obtain its much valued meat, who are the true enemy.

D to 000. Report received. The Organisation will expect you to reimburse it for the loss of one camera. *Message ends.*

OPERATION MINERVA:

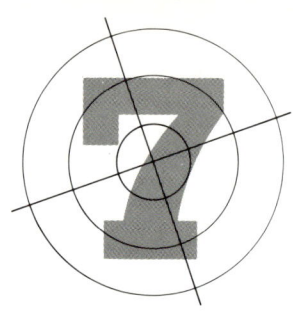

NAME □ Cuban Crocodile

ALIASES □ *Crocodylus rhombifer*, Cocodrilo de Cuba.

REPORTED SEEN □ Map ref E6

BACKGROUND □ **DANGER.** **DANGER.** The target is the rarest of all crocodilians, that ancient family of reptiles that includes crocodiles, alligators, ghavials and caimans – six of which are extremely dangerous man-eaters!

There are 25 species of crocodilian ranging in size from the 1 m long *Congo dwarf crocodile* to the fiercesome *saltwater crocodile*, perhaps the most dangerous of the lot, which can reach 6 and perhaps even 9 m in length.

Like all reptiles, crocodiles are 'cold-blooded' – their bodies are the same temperature as that of their immediate environment. They have heavily scaled skins and a muscular tail that is flattened from side to side and which is 'skulled' to push the animal through the water, while the limbs are tucked into the body. On land they can raise themselves up on their legs, with their body held well off the ground, and they can run quite fast. When they are not in the rivers, sluggish streams and lakes (and in the case of the saltwater crocodile, sometimes the sea) where they live, they may be found hauled out on sand-bars and banks, basking in the sunshine with their huge jaws gaping widely – not to catch things, but in order to lose excess heat. They don't mind when birds enter their open mouths to pick bits of food from between their teeth. I suppose they regard them as useful living toothbrushes!

A crocodile with its living toothpick.

The saltwater crocodile is probably the most dangerous of all crocodiles.

There are many legends about the crocodile. The ancient Egyptians worshipped them as divine and made mummies of their dead bodies. They believed that the crocodile was the only animal with eyes covered by a thin transparent membrane (not true), that allowed it to see without being seen – something that surely only a god could do.

You will know why we refer to 'crocodile tears' – false displays of sadness. It was believed that crocodiles shed tears over their prey while in the act of devouring it. Shakespeare says in *Henry VI*, 'as the mournful crocodile, with sorrow snares relenting passengers'. Funnily enough, there may be a grain of truth in this. When a croc has torn a large chunk of flesh off its victim and is swallowing it, pressure is exerted on the rather thin and flexible roof of the back of the reptile's mouth. This squeezes the tear glands which lie just above so that tears well up into the

eyelids and spill over. Crocodile tears, like those of humans, contain an antiseptic chemical which protects the eye from infection, particularly valuable to creatures who live in muddy water.

Another legend refers to crocodiles eating their young. This may arise from the fact that when the baby crocodiles hatch, their mother takes them very gently into her jaws and shakes them down into the pouched floor of her mouth. Then she carries them down to the water and sometimes swims with a mouthful of a dozen or more snappy little youngsters peeping out from between her teeth.

Other locations where it can be seen □
Zoos in HAVANA (Cuba) and elsewhere.

Estimated degree of survival threat □
Orange-red.

From the British Ambassador, Havana, to **D**. Top Security Code. Channel 86 scrambled telex. 23 March. 11.04 hrs. My staff have visited one of your field operatives detained by Cuban Intelligence Service. What is going on? My intelligence officer knows nothing of any current operations involving your section. Out.

D to British Ambassador, Havana. 23 March. 15.00 hrs. TOP SECURITY CODE. Channel 86 scrambled telex. Many apologies. Will explain next time you are back in UK when we can have a drink. Out.

One of the differences between a crocodile and an alligator is the way the fourth lower tooth fits into the lower jaw.

Field report from 000 to D.
Top Priority. Operation Minverva.
28 March. 06.15 hrs.
Had a spot of trouble when exploring the swampland of Cienaga de Zapata in central Cuba, a small area which is the last refuge of the *Cuban crocodile* in the wild. I was arrested by a patrol of Cuban soldiers and interrogated for six days. They thought I was a spy and refused to believe that The Organisation is purely concerned with endangered animals. Eventually the guy in charge said, 'So you claim to be nothing more than a keen biologist, *not* a spy – if that's the truth, prove it! Tell me – what is the main difference between a crocodile and an alligator?'

Was I relieved! Quick as a flash I told him – the fourth tooth on the lower jaw of an alligator fits neatly into a pit formed for it in the upper jaw, not into a notch at the side of the jaw as in crocodiles. Also, an alligator head is broader and shorter than a croc's and it doesn't have the jagged fringe that you'll find on the hind legs and feet of a crocodile. He checked with some professor and then I was free! Here is my delayed field report:

The Cuban crocodile can now only be found in this one small swamp. Although not one of the biggest crocodilians, it can grow up to around 4 m long and is very stocky and muscular, with teeth that are tilted outwards. It is undoubtedly the most bad tempered and aggressive species, and in the past, when it was more numerous, has attacked and killed human beings on occasion. But it has nothing like the reputation of other crocodiles such as the saltwater crocodile that probably kills 2-3,000 people per year or

Alligator

Crocodile

A surprisingly good mother, a female Nile crocodile carries her babies gently in her mouth.

the *Nile crocodile* which kills about 1,000 and has been known to take on horses and even big rhinoceroses which were drinking at the water's edge.

Crocodiles stalk their prey, watching with those cold eyes that protrude just above the water surface, swimming in stealthily and then suddenly launching an attack. The victim is seized – a croc's bite is 60 times stronger than that of the strongest man – and with furious twisting and shaking movements of its body, the reptile takes its prey down through the water. More twisting and spinning of its body tears limbs or large chunks of flesh from the unfortunate victim – a croc's teeth are for grabbing and holding, not slicing and chewing. Sometimes crocodiles put bodies into underwater 'larders', small caves or beneath boulders, for a few days where decomposition will soften them and make them easier to dismember. Normally, however, Cuban crocodiles eat fish, birds and any small mammals they can catch.

Like all crocodiles and alligators, Cuban crocodiles reproduce by laying eggs. The eggs are white and oval, rather like goose eggs, and they are laid in a mound of rotting vegetation where they incubate by the heat of fermentation of the 'compost'. The mother guards the nest from intruders, and scratches away the

vegetation covering the eggs when the youngsters call to her, making hiccup-like cries from within the egg, when they are ready to hatch! The babies cut their way out of the tough egg-shell by means of an 'egg-tooth' which they have on the tip of their snout, but which is lost soon after birth. Growth in crocodiles depends on environmental temperature and the amount of available food, but is usually about 0.3 m per year for the first few years and more slowly after that. They can live to a great age – some experts think as much as 200 years. *Message ends.*

D to 000. How many Cuban crocodiles do you estimate still to exist?

000 to D. A few hundred. Luckily the Cuban government has declared the swamp a sanctuary and the animals are effectively protected.

D to 000. Please identify enemies of the crocodile.

The closest living relatives of the dinosaur, a group of Cuban crocodiles bask in the sun.

000 to D. Re. crocodile enemies.
1. Man. The Cuban crocodile is probably safe, provided the swampland remains a sanctuary and is not drained in the future for agricultural or other development. In the past it was severely overhunted for its skin to make fancy leather goods. Other species of crocodile still suffer from hunters – crocodile skins continue to fetch very high prices. Controlled hunting and the setting up of crocodile farms can help to conserve these fascinating animals in the wild, but the numbers of some once-plentiful crocodiles are dropping steadily. No longer is the Nile crocodile to be found in Egypt – you remember that verse in *Alice in Wonderland* –

'How doth the little crocodile
Improve his shining tail,
And pour the waters of the Nile,
On every golden scale!'

OPERATION MINERVA: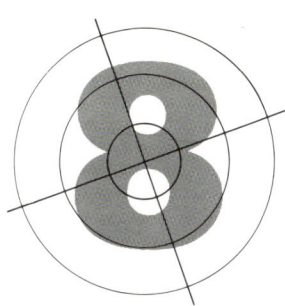

NAME □ **African Hunting Dog**

ALIASES □ African wild dog, Cape hunting dog, painted dog, tri-coloured dog.

REPORTED SEEN □ Map ref M9

BACKGROUND □ This is another mission that you should not underestimate, 000. A dog, yes, but an increasingly endangered species of dog and one that could easily soon become extinct. Normally, when folk talk of rare dogs, they are referring to *unusual breeds* of domestic dog like the Caes de Agua, the Loewchen or the Glen of Imaal, pedigree aristocrats that you rarely see at a small dog show alongside the popular labradors, German shepherds and poodles. And among wild dogs there are some little-known and rarely seen species such as the *bush dog* of South America and the *dhole* of Asia, though the most threatened species is the *hunting dog*, a native of Africa.

This dog is certainly the most carnivorous of all the canine family and typifies the cooperative, social, versatile and intelligent character that made the dogs such an evolutionary success. Where cats are highly specialised, often solitary, self-reliant hunters, dogs are animals of the pack, adaptable and not over-specialised in any aspect – qualities that have enabled them to spread over the planet to a great extent.

Both dogs and cats originated about 60 million years ago from a small, weasel-like animal with a long, flexible body, long tail and short legs, that lived in

Hunting dogs attack a gnu.

You can see why the hunting dog is sometimes called the 'painted' dog.

forests. Its name was *Miacis*.

The canid family of dogs, wolves, foxes, coyotes and jackals (perhaps the hunting dog's closest relatives) all have one thing in common – long, narrow heads with long jaws and plentiful teeth. The cheek teeth are adapted partly for slicing and partly for grinding and can efficiently handle both meat and vegetable foods. The African hunting dog's teeth emphasise the slicing functions and indeed it eats virtually nothing but raw meat.

Hunting dogs are rangy animals standing about as high as a pointer or Irish setter and weighing up to 35 kg. They have a very short, dark coat that bears irregular yellow, orange and white blotches in a pattern which is unique to each individual. The legs are long and greyhound-like and the tail ends in a bush tipped with white. The ears are large and rounded, helping to keep the dog cool by radiating heat.

Other locations where it can be seen □
Zoos at PORT LYMPNE (UK) and in USA.

Estimated degree of survival threat □
Red.

Field report from 000 to D.
Top priority. Operation Minerva.
11 April. 14.45 hrs.
My landrover was overturned by a charging rhino this morning and as a result my

radio is out of action. This report comes to you courtesy of the British High Commission radio room in the capital.

It was not easy to locate the target species, undoubtedly because they are greatly reduced in numbers, often with no more than one pack per 2,000 sq. km of countryside.

Miacis, ancestor of the dog family, lived many millions of years ago.

The hunting dogs form packs of 2-32 animals with an average of about a dozen, though packs of up to 50 have been recorded. Long ago packs perhaps numbered hundreds. They travel longer distances than wolves, covering up to 50 km a day over their hunting territory which may be perhaps 40 sq. km in area when game is plentiful, but expand to 200 sq. km when it is scarce.

The pack does everything together – hunting, travelling and resting, and each individual works for the common good. As hunters, they do not depend on stalking, ambushing or the single-handed fast, but brief, attack, like the tiger or leopard. The hunting dog strategy is one of cooperation and stamina.

The dogs can keep up a chase for long distances. First one member of the pack will lead in pursuing the prey, and then, as he begins to flag, another will move up to the front. The chase continues relentlessly with the dogs being able to keep going at 48 kmh for over 5 km and, if necessary, accelerating for short bursts up to 55 kmh. They hunt by sight, recognising each of their comrades by their individual coat patterns, and signalling with their large, mobile ears. Using such hunting methods, they can bring down much larger animals like zebras and eland, and on occasion they have been known to tire out and kill a lone lion. Their main prey are small antelopes and gazelle, particularly Thomson's gazelle, and they also catch rodents and other small mammals.

Hunting dog packs have an unusual social structure with separate 'pecking orders' of males and females, each ruled

A pack of hunting dogs chase a gazelle.

Hunting dogs working together will sometimes take on a solitary lion.

by one top dog – a 'king' and a 'queen'. All of the males, and likewise the females, are related to one another; but only the 'queen' is related to any of the males. The 'queen' alone is allowed to breed and raise a litter of pups. Other females' litters are normally killed by the 'queen'. Males born and allowed to survive stay with the pack for their entire lives – generally shorter than those of domestic dogs at about ten years. Females stay until they are between one and two and a half years of age and then leave as a group to join a separate pack.

The packs look after the lucky pups very thoughtfully, staying near the den where they are born until they are old enough at about three months to go a-roaming with the adults. When they are weaned at nine to ten weeks, the pups are protected and supplied with food by members of the pack as a whole. *Message ends.*

D to 000. I await your detailed explanation of your squabble with the rhino with much interest when you return. How many African hunting dogs do you estimate still to exist?

000 to D. Probably only a few thousand now – a dramatic reduction in recent years. Once they were to be found almost everywhere in the continent. Now many packs are isolated.

D to 000. Please identify enemies of the African hunting dog.

000 to D. Re. African hunting dog enemies.

1. Man. (a) By persecuting the dogs themselves.
   (b) Diminishing habitat due to the expansion of human populations and activities.
2. Drastic reduction in the numbers of some prey animals such as springbok from various causes, in southern Africa.
3. Serious epidemics of the disease which domestic dogs are vaccinated against – distemper.

In some areas where they still exist they have legal protection and some packs do live in national parks like the Serengeti.

OPERATION MINERVA: 9

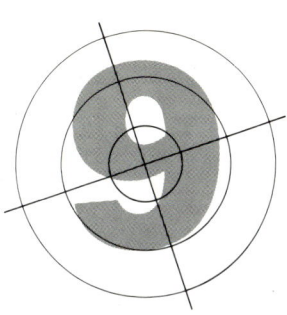

NAME □ **Lemurs**

ALIASES □ Various local and scientific names.

REPORTED SEEN □ Map ref N9

BACKGROUND □ The Romans gave the name *lemur* to the spirits of the dead and believed there were two kinds, the good ones, *lares,* and the terrifyingly bad ones, *larvae*. The delightful animals that have inherited the name *lemur* were regarded as mysterious, ghost-like creatures by the first humans with whom they came into contact, both natives and early European explorers of their island home.

There are accounts of men with dog's heads in many civilisations. Marco Polo said that these people lived on the Andaman Islands in the Indian Ocean. In Byzantine art, St Christopher is often depicted with a canine head and the legend runs that the saint was so uncommonly handsome that he prayed

One of the most comical sights in nature, an indri lemur walking along.

A ring-tailed lemur leaping through the trees.

to God to give him a dog's head to stop the girls pursuing him. The medieval Sir John Mandeville wrote of dog-men inhabiting an island which he called Macumera. Very possibly he was referring to the place where you will seek your target, for there is one species of lemur, the large *indri*, which does possess a rather dog-like head and a very human-like body.

Lemurs, of course, are not dogs, but primates like you and me. They are so called 'lower primates', being less advanced than man, the three great apes and monkeys. The lower primates have smaller brains in proportion to their body size, and longer snouts on their faces. They possess a better sense of smell, but do not have the ability to see a broad spectrum of colours, like we more advanced primates.

All species of lemur – there are at present 23, including one discovered only in 1987 – live in the same large island of Madagascar and nowhere else. They range in size from one of the smallest of all primates, the *grey lesser mouse lemur* that weighs a mere 45-80 g and is 27-30 cm long, including the tail, to the 10 kg indri. One of the rarest of all primates is the *hairy-eared dwarf lemur*, the first live specimen of which was found just over 20 years ago.

Lemurs are furry creatures with long, often bushy tails and fore limbs (arms) that are distinctly shorter than the hind limbs (legs). The coat colours of different species are varied – some being more or less monochrome grey or brown, while others sport zones of two contrasting colours, black and white or black and red, for example. All have black muzzles with a damp nosepad, and an array of sensitive whiskers.

Lemurs are great sniffers and smellers, using scent produced by scent glands in their skin to communicate with one another. Other methods of communication between these animals are visual and vocal. Some have striking

signal designs on their body, like the *ring-tailed lemur* with distinct black and grey-white bands on its tail, and they can utter a variety of calls.

Other locations where they can be seen □
Many zoos including LONDON, TWYCROSS, EDINBURGH, (UK) SAN DIEGO, WASHINGTON, (USA) etc.

Estimated degree of survival threat □
Yellow to red.

Field report from 000 to D.
Top priority. Operation Minerva.
16 May. 06.00 hrs.
Please forgive any garbling of this report. Having difficulty speaking after being stung on lower lip by a very aggressive African hornet.

Have located various species of the target animal, but some are exceedingly rare and difficult to track down, particularly the nocturnal kinds. Once there were many more species of lemur on the island, including one as big as an orang-outang. The evolution of lemurs is a fascinating story; it seems that their ancestors came to the island, perhaps on mats of floating vegetation, some 50 million years ago. Separated from their fellows on the huge continent nearby, they then evolved in their own unique way. But then, of course, it had to happen! Man the hunter arrived on the island. He started to establish settlements there about 2,000 years ago. The rich collection of lemurs, some rather like koala bears, others baboon-like and still others rather gibbonish, soon started to suffer. Man's fire destroyed the forest habitat and his domestic animals competed with and harassed the lemurs. He also considered them an excellent source of food.

Surviving lemurs are forest-dwellers with only the ring-tailed lemur (the sort most commonly seen in zoos) spending much time on the ground. All are vegetarians who pick leaves, young shoots and fruits. One, the *mongoose lemur*, also gathers sweet nectar from flowers; the dwarf and mouse lemurs eat lots of insects; and the dwarf lemurs also collect gum (not bubble-gum!) from trees.

Some species are active during the day, others at night, and still others keep busy in spells around the clock. The nocturnal types have large eyes with a light-gathering 'mirror' of cells containing shiny crystals set behind the retina of their eyes.

Lemur society varies according to the species. Some lead fairly solitary lives (i.e. the *sportive lemur*), others live as strongly-bonded pairs together with their offspring (i.e. the mongoose lemur) and many form bigger groups of 5-35 animals (i.e. the ring-tailed lemur).

The tiniest lemurs are the ones we know least about. They are totally tree-

The charming mongoose lemur.

The strange and persecuted aye-aye.

dwelling, night workers who often make nests out of leaves.

The biggest lemurs are day-workers and to me the most fascinating is the indri. It is called 'babakoto' in the local language and in the old legends of the island is said to be man's ancestor. It often sits in a posture rather like that of a human being, and when it hops along the ground with its arms held outstretched to the sides or above its head, with the body tilted backwards and its tummy thrust forwards, it does make a comic impersonation of a rather tipsy ballet dancer or high-wire artiste.

The oddest of all the lemur group is the solitary and nocturnal *aye-aye*. This strange creature has a thick brown coat sprinkled with white hairs, big ears, long front teeth and a very long middle finger on each hand. It feeds on hard-shelled fruits such as coconut – that's why it needs the long teeth to deal with the shell and the long finger to scoop out the contents! The large ears are useful for listening out for the grubs which it also loves to eat, as they squirm about under the tree bark.

The aye-aye is almost extinct, not just because of the destruction of its habitat, but also because local people, noting its strange witch-like finger, vampirish teeth and overall weird appearance, consider it a devilish beast and kill it. *Message ends.*

D to 000. Please identify enemies of the lemur.

000 to D. Re. enemies of the lemur.
1. Man. Habitat destruction to produce timber and land for agriculture. Some species are trapped and shot for eating. Some of the more specialised species like the *gentle lemur*, which depend on supplies of bamboo, are at more imminent risk than others which have more flexible diets and lifestyle. There are protected areas on the island, but they cover only a very small part of the total lemur territory. It is to be hoped that such zones can be increased in size and number and that the well thought out management schemes can be expanded.

OPERATION MINERVA: 10

NAME □ Gorilla

ALIAS □ *Gorilla gorilla*

REPORTED SEEN □ Map ref L7

BACKGROUND □ In about 500 BC, the Carthaginian navigator, Hanno, wrote of his voyage of exploration to the west coast of Africa. He reported the existence there of an animal allegedly called 'gorilla' by the natives and that name was eventually adopted by scientists in Europe in the mid-nineteenth century.

The largest of the three anthropoid (man-like) apes, the *gorilla* had, until recently the undeserved reputation of a wild thug or ruffian of the jungle. The 1933 film *King Kong*, based on a novel by Edgar Wallace, in which a giant gorilla terrorises the city of New York, contributed to the myth of the animals' aggressiveness. What nonsense!

Although without doubt a mighty, muscle-rippling beast that can tip the scales at up to 275 kg (Phil, a gorilla at

Gorillas are now seriously threatened.

St Louis Zoo, who died in 1958, was claimed to have weighed a spectacular 352 kg!), standing taller than most men at a little over 2 m and boasting a chest measurement of 170 cm, an arm span of 2.7 m and 63 cm biceps, the gorilla is in fact a shy, peaceable and delightful character. In my experience, he is far less dangerous than the mercurial and immensely strong adult chimpanzee.

Of all the targets in your current mission, the gorilla is the one which, in my view, is most likely to vanish from its old haunts during our lifetime.

Gorillas are heavily built apes, closely related to chimpanzees, but much bigger and with different bodily proportions. A big crest of bone running from back to front along the top of the skull is particularly pronounced in male gorillas and produces the high head so distinctive of these animals. Gorillas have much smaller ears than chimps and nostrils which are surrounded by broad ridges of hairless, shiny skin.

There are three races of gorilla. The *mountain gorilla* is the largest of the three and, as its name suggests, lives in tropical forests up to an altitude of about 3,800 m. Its hair is rather longer than the others and is black with a silvery 'saddle' on the back of mature males.

The *Eastern lowland gorilla* is similar to the mountain gorilla but with shorter hair and somewhat longer arms.

The *Western lowland gorilla* has a coat of greyish-brown and the silvery saddle of the male extends the buttocks and upper thighs.

Other locations where they can be seen □

Many zoos such as HOWLETT'S, CHESSINGTON, LONDON (UK), SAN DIEGO (USA), etc.

Estimated degree of survival threat □

Red. Particularly the mountain gorilla.

Field report from 000 to D.

Top priority. Operation Minerva.
2 July. 13.00 hrs.

I am exhausted! The rainforest is incredibly hard going and I have been plagued by mosquitoes as big as elephants. Nevertheless, true to the traditions of The Organisation, I have achieved my objectives. The targets have been located.

The Western lowland gorilla lives in the region of map ref L10 while the Eastern lowland and mountain races inhabit bamboo and higher altitude rainforests about 1,000 km to the east at map ref N8.

Gorillas are strict vegetarians feeding on a variety of leaves, shoots, herbs and some fruit. Not for them the occasional meat meal like the chimpanzees who will kill and devour monkeys and birds. They

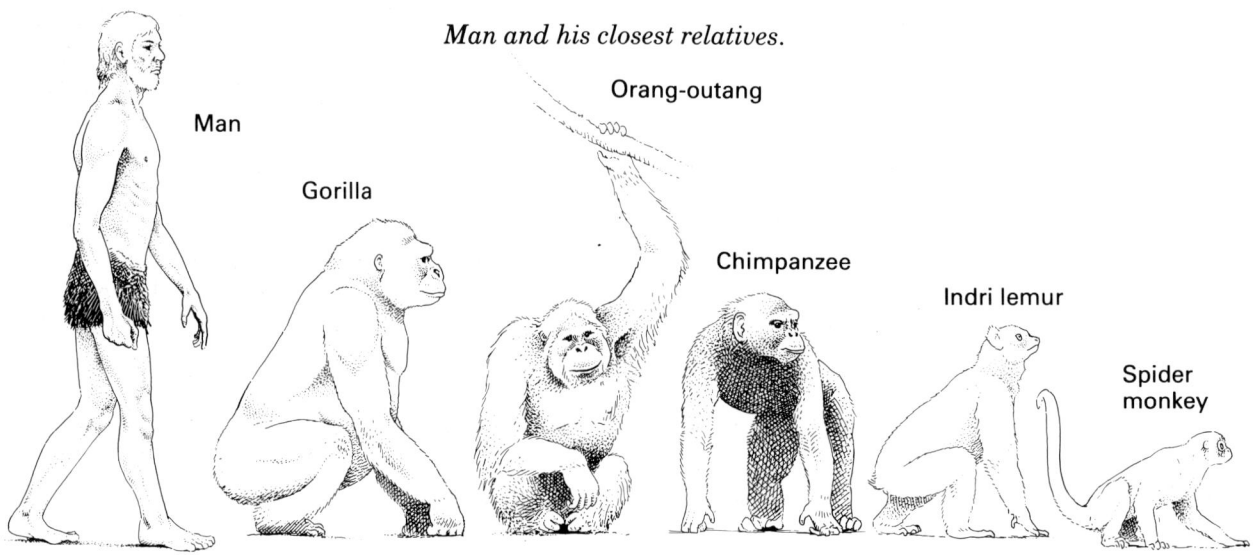

Man and his closest relatives.

Mum's back is the perfect spot for a baby gorilla's nap.

form permanent groups of about a dozen animals including youngsters, with a big male as leader. Sometimes groups of 30 or more have been recorded.

The gorillas are active by day and build nests in trees or lower vegetation at night by pulling branches and leaves down into a rough hammock. They feed in the morning, rest during the greatest heat in the middle of the day, and then feed again during the late afternoon. Each day the troop travels a short distance of 0.5-1 km within their territories which cover an area of 5-30 sq. km. Where gorillas live there is plenty of food and thus they do not need to travel far to gather their meals, and although one can speak of territories belonging to particular gorilla troops, there is no defence of these areas, and much overlapping of territories occurs without outbreaks of warfare or even proprietorial indignation.

Baby gorillas are born at any time of the year after a pregnancy of 251-289 days. They weigh about 2 kg at birth. They begin to crawl at about two months of age and can walk at about seven to ten months. They wean when they are around two and a half years old. Sadly – but that is nature's way – about one in three young gorillas don't reach their third birthday.

Gorillas are not aggressive and don't fight or indulge in inter-tribal battles like chimpanzees. Sometimes a leading male gorilla will drive off another male with awesome-looking displays of bellicose behaviour – charging, chest-beating and roaring – but it's almost always theatre, an impressive display of bluff, and it seldom gets serious.

The same applies to gorilla/human encounters. You might be subjected to the showy bluff that I've just mentioned, but it is very rare indeed for a gorilla physically to harm a human being unless it feels that its family group is in some way being threatened. We have little to fear from gorillas; they have much to fear from us. *Message ends.*

D to 000. How many gorillas do you estimate still to exist?

000 to D. Perhaps about 11,000, of which fewer than 300 are mountain gorillas.

D to 000. Please identify enemies of the gorilla.

000 to D. Re. Gorilla enemies.
1. Man. The destruction of habitat. Forest is being cleared to provide timber and make way for agriculture, including domestic livestock.
2. Man. Gorillas are killed by the local population because they sometimes raid crops such as plantations of bananas.
3. Man. Some people kill gorillas to eat them. I have located restaurants in towns such as Libreville where gorilla steaks are on the menu!

The threatening display of a gorilla is more for show than for real.

A gorilla carefully grooms a youngster.

4. Man. Until recently many adult gorillas were killed so that the young could be taken for sale to zoos and the pet trade. Spain and Belgium were particularly bad at allowing the import trade in baby gorillas to flourish. Only a remnant of disreputable zoos in certain countries would nowadays accept such unfortunate contra band animals.

5. Man. Gorillas are still killed to provide disgusting curios for the tourist trade. Gorilla skulls, hands and feet are sold to a certain kind of stupid and unprincipled person.

Conservation and protection schemes for gorillas exist to varying degrees in most countries where the animal exists. The difficulty is enforcing these laws in lands where the terrain is so difficult to police and where other human problems can lay claim to scarce resources or money, skill and manpower. Perhaps, following the success worldwide of the film *Gorillas In The Mist* people will begin to value the gorilla more, to realise that it is an important citizen of its country and that it could help to bring in much-needed cash, not by killing it or driving it from the forest, but by stimulating informed and well-run tourism.

D to 000. Well done. Mission accomplished. Return to base. Your information invaluable in the fight to protect the target animals. First the good news – you can take one week's leave. Second, the bad news – I have a list of another ten target animals for you to investigate after that.

Message from D to all agents ☐
Top priority. All agents who write to the following address: Boxtree Limited, 36 Tavistock Street, London WC2E 7PB, enclosing a stamped addressed envelope, and mentioning the password 'Owl-Hoot' will receive a personally signed dossier listing the 50 most endangered animals in the world from 'D'. Mark the envelope 'Top secret – animals in danger'.

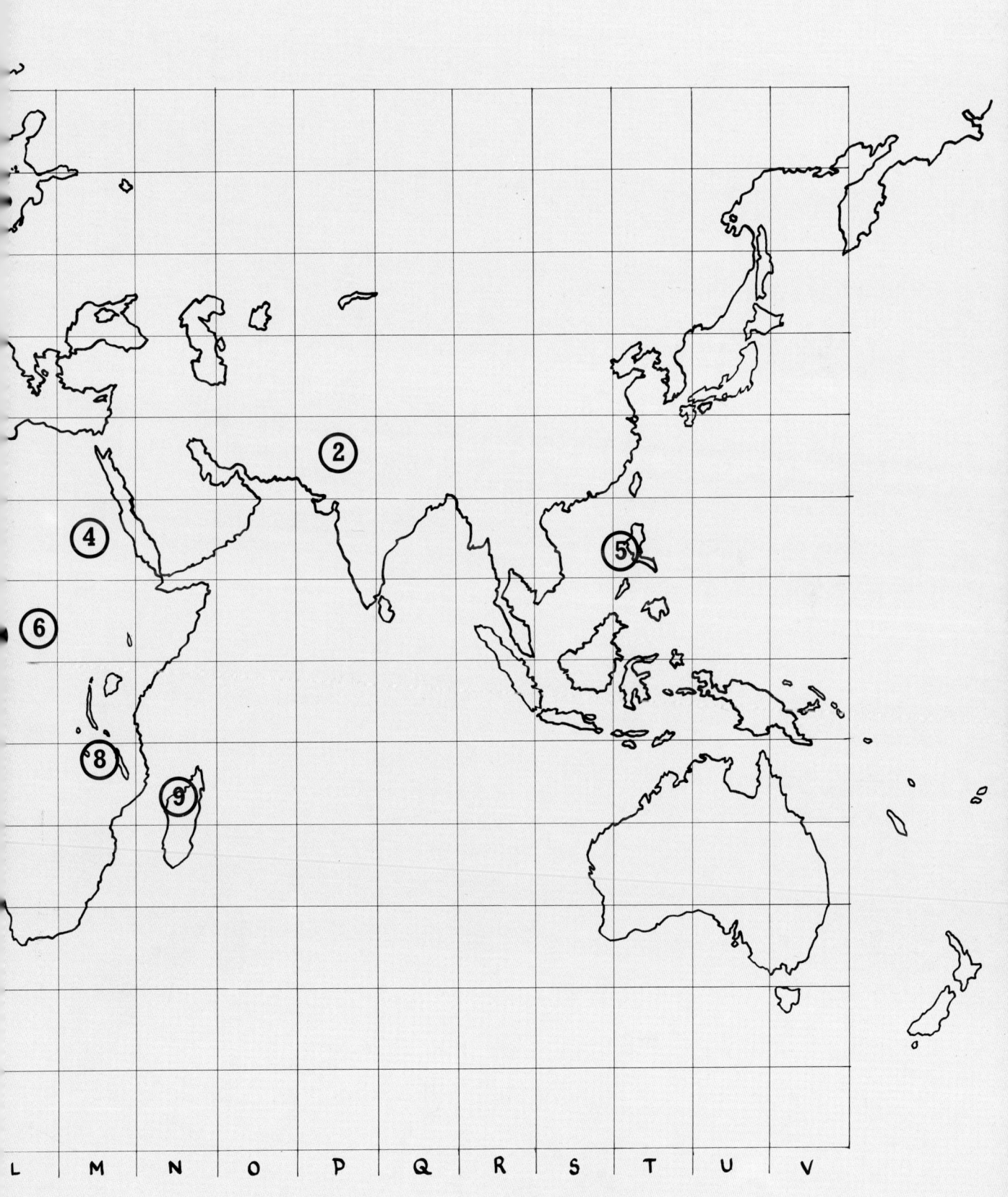